Dearest Pam,

You are such beautiful soul! May you continue to find the love of self and stand in your power and be the beacon of light & strength for yourself and all in your presence.

Always!

Melissa

LESSONS *of* MANY LIVES

How looking to past (lives) helped me find my past,
cherish my present and shape my future

LESSONS *of* MANY LIVES

How looking to past (lives) helped me find my past,
cherish my present and shape my future

MELISSA WATTS
with KAREN FRAZIER

Wasteland Press
Shelbyville, KY USA
www.wastelandpress.net

Lessons of Many Lives
by Melissa Watts

Second Printing—March 2014
ISBN: 978-1-60047-328-9

Printed in the U.S.A.

0   1   2   3   4

To my guide, ALL – who has been and is my guiding light.
And to all of the guides of everyone who has found
their way here. Thank you for bringing them.
We have an appointment with destiny.

life's promise
lies in listening
to the deep yearning from within
breathe in
be
believe
know
the truth has never left you
you are being guided

TABLE OF CONTENTS

Acknowledgements

FOREWORD

I met Lisa on a freelance writing bid site. Those aren't always very friendly places to be, but I didn't know that at the time. I was just starting out as I transitioned from a job in corporate America to working my passion as a full-time writer. My vision had not yet taken shape. I knew I wanted to write. I knew I was good at it. But I assumed that I would have to write about things that I didn't care about, didn't love, and didn't believe in. I had to make a living, you see. And unfortunately, those things that earn money are often not the same things that drive our passions. Or so I thought.

It was a simple ad. Write web content for a hypnotherapist's website. That was certainly something I could do. Not only that, it was something that I might even enjoy.

You see, I've always had an interest in things that others might perceive as just a little bit different. My main writing gig is for a paranormal magazine, and I love the subject matter. I more than love the subject matter. I am compelled to learn more about it. I never really understood why I had that compulsion and that interest. I just knew that I had it.

So, there I was. Mostly unemployed and on a freelance bid site staring down a request for a copywriter. About hypnotherapy, no less, something I had just undergone for the purpose of writing a magazine article on Past Life Regression. I submitted my bid and mentioned my article. Heck – I sent my article. Somehow, I knew deep inside, that I would get the job.

I did.

Lisa and I had nearly an instant connection – despite the continent that is between us. We've only spoken on the phone, but I can tell you that I know Lisa. I felt as if I knew her instantly.

It is more than common ground. I connected with her through a few words on a computer screen. I knew as soon as I saw them that I would work with her, and I did.

As we worked on her website, which happened easily and quickly – almost as if we didn't even need to think about it – I mentioned writing a book. And this book was born.

Lisa has become my friend. Or, more accurately, Lisa is my friend and was my friend before I even met her. She has an openness and an outlook that works well with my more closed, pessimistic nature. She is afraid of nothing, and she has total trust in the universe. That nature is what I have always reached for, but never grasped.

There have always been things I know intellectually, but that I've never really internalized. I've always known that I should trust. I've never quite trusted. I have chased faith all of my life, but never quite found it. I've always known that I want to be a light, but I've never quite have been able to open myself up to be that. It's been wheel spinning at its finest.

Lisa's story, and Lisa herself, has been instrumental in helping me to change all of that. My wheels may still be spinning, but I think they're gaining traction. As we've gone through the process of writing this book, I've begun to trust.

It started with small things. The knowing that I would be chosen to write Lisa's website. How easily the words have come to write this amazing story. The recognition I feel as I hear of Lisa's experiences. A little bit of trust goes a long way towards building a lot of trust.

This book is about Lisa's journey. But my journey – and yours, too, if you are open to it – is intertwined with the words on these pages. As I write this book, I have started to pay attention. I have started to listen and my world has begun to open up.

I realize now that my interest in the paranormal has always been about one thing: my search for faith. I've spent a lot of time in a faith vacuum, envying those who have faith and wishing somehow that I could find what they have. But I was looking in the wrong places.

Here's what I've learned. Faith isn't found in an event. It isn't found in an external source. Everything we have, everything we need, everything we are – the keys to those things exist only in one place. The truth of who we are exists inside of each of us. Not the small us that we recognize as our human selves, but the huge, expansive us that exist as souls who are all connected to one another and everything else.

Not bad for a freelancing bid site. I believe – no, I know – that I was led there for this purpose. I found more than a writing job. I found faith. Best paycheck I ever received.

~Karen Frazier
April 6, 2009
Chehalis, Washington

INTRODUCTION

My life has been profoundly affected by past life regression hypnotherapy. As a matter of fact, the effects have been so powerful and far-reaching in my life that I became a hypnotherapist out of a desire to help others experience the same deep insights that I have had.

It took me nearly 40 years to find my place in this world – but not for lack of seeking. Most of my life, I felt like there was something out there just beyond my reach, just waiting for me to embrace it.

I used to browse in bookstores searching for that one thing that would help bring deeper meaning into my life. I read and explored everything, seeking answers. I found some interesting information, but nothing that resonated deeply with who I was.

I was looking for a way to make sense of everything, and I was stuck.

Then, one day, a book literally jumped off of the shelf, and that book deeply touched my soul. It was the catalyst that would begin a series of events that changed my life forever. Yet, it was more than ten years later before it all started to come together. It wasn't until I found my way into the office of hypnotherapist, Paul Aurand that everything fell into place in remarkable ways. Now that I am on my path, I want to help others find theirs.

If you are trapped in relationships and in patterns that you don't understand or have a deep curiosity and sense that there is more to life – I can relate to those feelings. If you feel stuck in your life and feel like there is a deeper meaning and purpose to life, you are not alone.

I have experienced all of those feelings. I didn't understand my life, my relationships or my place in the universe. Until one day, I gave way to destiny.

And now, I want to help others truly experience the joy of connection that comes when everything finally falls into place.

All of my life, I have been searching, longing to receive something that I could not explain. Now... having realized the gift of my life's purpose, I extend myself, and I am compelled to pass it on to others. If you are searching and you have found your way to this book, then the universe is knocking at your door. Your own unique answer – or the key to finding that answer – may well lie within the pages of this book. The information has come through me for you. I am not the source. I am merely the conduit.

I am a firm believer that what we need is provided when you are ready. Our job is to pay attention so that we don't miss it when it is presented to us.

This is your moment. What you take away from it is up to you. You will know what you need, it will resonate so deeply in your soul; you will not be able to ignore it. When you are ready, open and truthful, you will be compelled to follow your heart and find the meaning you seek, much as I found mine.

Thank you for allowing me to be part of your journey.

~Melissa Watts
March 1, 2009

Before I Knew

Life is a promise; fulfill it.
~Mother Theresa

CHAPTER 1

The Secret Girl

I have always known innately that there is something more to life than what we experience on this earth. While everyone grows up feeling that they are special or different from everyone else, I felt a sense of separation from the rest of the world. I was shrouded by the secret life that I lived inside of my mind.

Even as a child, I knew there was something that I was supposed to do in this life. From my earliest memories, I was seeking answers to the questions that I never allowed myself to verbalize to the people around me. I led a double life from birth.

On the outside, I was a normal kid. I was active and involved in life. I was close to my family, and I had lots of friends. But inside, I was the secret girl. I lived a secret life that I was afraid to share with anyone – not even those closest to me. None of the people in my inner circle knew who I was at my deepest core.

I was the girl who went to the library and asked for the metaphysical and paranormal section. In New York in the 1970s, this often raised eyebrows with the librarians, who gave me a strange look before pointing me to a tiny section at the back of the library.

I spent hours in the library absorbing any information I came across about ghosts, hauntings, numerology, psychics and astrology. I pored over anything I could find that helped me feed the hunger I had for information about those parts of ourselves that no one really talked about or understood.

Meanwhile, at home I was a different child. I kept my library missions to myself. The only person in my family who knew of my burning interest in the paranormal and metaphysical was my sister, Tina. She kept my secret.

One of the things I remember the most about being a child is feeling and remembering the vibrations of others. I have vague memories of being very young and crawling around in diapers noticing the vibrational signature of people.

Let me back up a moment to explain. As far back as I can remember each person I have encountered has had a unique energetic feel to them. Think of it this way. When you think of someone you love, or when you are in their presence, do you have a certain feeling that is attached only to that person? If so, you are likely picking up on their subtle vibrational energy. It is easiest to tune into the vibrations of those that we love, but if you pay careful attention, you may be able to develop this sense and start to feel the vibrations of all of the people around you.

So it was with me. From my very earliest memories, even before I had words to describe what I was feeling, I was aware of how people felt to me vibrationally. Everyone's vibration told the story of that person.

As I grew up and started to think and express myself in words, I found that I still didn't pay much attention to the physical aspects of the person. While some people may recognize people through their physical senses – how they look, smell, sound and feel to the touch – I was a little different. What I connected with people and what I remembered about them was their energetic signature.

Through this inner sense that I had, I could learn a lot about the people with whom I interacted. Everyone's vibration told the story of that person. I could also pick up the vibrations of an environment, which gave me an innate understanding of the dynamics of situations long before I had a context in which to place them. Because of this, I learned at a very early age the whole spectrum of human emotion. I also had an uncanny sense of situational awareness.

I kept my inner world such a secret that the adults in my life weren't aware of how tuned in I was to everyone and everything. I was extremely lucky, however, because even though my parents weren't aware of how much I understood about everything that was going on, they gave me such a strong foundation of love that I was instinctively able to make sense of emotions and situations that were probably well beyond my developmental capacity to understand.

I thought everyone was like me. Since I naturally tuned into the vibrations of others, I assumed that everyone else did the same thing. This may be why I didn't share my inner self with others – because by the time I figured out that everyone else wasn't like me, I decided that if they knew, they might react to me unfavorably.

CHAPTER 2

Always in the Middle

I was always in the middle of EVERYTHING. No matter what happened, if it was big and dramatic, it seemed that I was there at the center of it.

As a child, I was always looking to others to create a definition of myself – as children so often do. I was no different. Except that in my extreme sensitivity to the vibrational energy of others, coupled with my uncanny situational awareness, much of what I picked up on in my self-definition came from undercurrents and unspoken emotions.

What I learned from those around me is that I had some kind of a calming energy that immediately soothed situations. As soon as I figured this out, it became my unspoken self-definition. I took it on myself to be there, to be in the middle, and to be a calming influence. It was how I knew to connect with others.

I remember when I was very young – just four or five years old, I was with my grandmother. She had been out drinking with friends. When she got home, a family member called and said that she was going to drink a bottle of Clorox and kill herself.

Grandma was tired, and because she'd been drinking, she was in no position to be driving a car. But she also had a friend in need, and she had to go save her. So, we hopped in the car and headed out to the relative's house.

Grandma was upset, tired and tipsy. At the tender age of four or five, I already knew what my job was, though. I was there to calm and comfort her. And to help her drive. I have a vivid recollection of taking the wheel as we drove down a one-way street, steering the car. I was in the middle, and I was there as a source of calm.

Another example of finding myself in the middle of things comes from when I was probably ten or eleven. My parents gave my sister, Tina, and me swimming lessons at the local pool. Tina was out swimming in the middle of the pool when she started to struggle.

She panicked, and couldn't make it to the side. She was drowning, and none of the instructors saw what was happening. Even though I was small and not the strongest of swimmers, I somehow managed to get to my sister, and I kept her calm. I helped her to float the edge of the pool.

I got Tina up on the side of the pool, and was able to help her expel the water that was in her lungs. All without a single grown-up noticing that it had happened.

Once again, I was in the right place at the right time and instinctively knew how to do what needed to be done.

That day, as with my grandmother years before, something or someone was guiding me and helping me to do what needed to be done to generate the best possible outcome.

And so it went throughout much of my childhood. When things were disharmonious, I felt that it was my responsibility to hold it together for everyone involved. In this way, I was a miniature adult. I took on the responsibility because it was how I knew to present myself in the world.

Knowing what to do and how to do it was innate. Even from a young age, I know I was guided.

CHAPTER 3

If Not For My Father

My father was my anchor. If spirit guides can manifest as human beings, it was and is my father. If they speak through the people in our lives, then mine spoke to me through my father.

Dad worked for NYPD. All of my life, I knew him to be hard working, loving and kind. He was also a philosopher. His way of presenting in the world was to be exactly who he was, at all times. He shared many of the same interests that I kept to myself, but unlike me, he wasn't ashamed to tell anyone of them.

Perhaps that part of him recognized the part of me that I didn't talk about. Or, maybe he just wanted to share his interests with one of his children. Whatever the reason, it was as if my father instinctively knew how to keep that spark of interest alive and burning inside of me.

Whether it was a book he gave me to read, or something he said, my dad was the source of much that nurtured me in my quest for whatever it was I was seeking. And those things that he gave nourished me in my silence.

The first book that I remember Dad giving me that really resonated was *One Flew Over the Cuckoo's Nest*. He gave that to me when I was in the fourth or fifth grade, and then he followed it up with books that spoke to the core of my being, like Jane Robert's *Seth Speaks*, Wayne Dyer's *Erroneous Zones* and Lama Govinda's *The Way of the White Clouds*.

Each of these books was like food for my soul, and I filled up my spiritual tanks with these offerings of love from my father.

If not for him, I'm not sure that I would have been as grounded in my childhood as I was. And, if not for him, I'm not sure I would have so willingly and joyfully followed my path when it was finally presented to me.

In recognizing and nurturing that secret part of my soul, my father gave me a gift. He let me know that my secret girl was not only okay, but that she was welcome and loved. Thanks, Dad.

CHAPTER 4

The Week That Changed My World-View

When I was seventeen, everything changed. It started the weekend of Mother's Day.

I had a childhood sweetheart. We met in elementary school. We dated off and on growing up, and were always close. As teenagers, we didn't go to the same high school, and we weren't together anymore, but I always had strong feelings for him. You always carry a torch for your first love, and I was certainly no different with Joseph.

On Mothers' Day, he showed up at my house at about three or four in the afternoon and asked if I wanted to go for a ride on his motorcycle.

I was seeing someone else at the time, so I told him that I didn't think I should go out with him. He was insistent. When I wouldn't go, he told me that he'd come pick me up tomorrow after school instead, and that we'd go for ice cream. Then he left. It was he last time I saw him.

The next day at school, one of my girlfriends came up and asked me if I'd heard that he had died. I thought that he was getting back at me for not going for a ride with him the day before, and I just sort of laughed it off and headed to class.

Later that day, another mutual friend stopped me in the hallway and asked if I'd heard that he had died the previous afternoon in a motorcycle accident. He told me that there was a girl named Lisa on the back of his bike at the time.

I was starting to get angry now at the lengths that he was going to in order to get even with me about not going out with him the day before. I didn't for a moment stop to think that it might be true.

At the end of the day, one of my close friends came up to me in the hallway and told me that it was true – that he had died in a motorcycle accident shortly after he left my house the day before. It was a hit and run.

I went home in shock. I don't think it had hit me yet. I called his mom, and she confirmed that he had been killed the previous day in a hit and run.

When the numbness wore off, I was absolutely devastated. Here was a vibrant eighteen-year-old whose life that had been snuffed out. One day, he was at my door – vibrant, handsome, and a really good, kind person. The next moment, he was gone. All of his plans for the future died with him, a month short of his high school graduation.

I don't know that I've ever before or since experienced the level of despair that I felt learning of his death. It pushed me to a place where I started to question many things. I wondered where he was now that he was no longer alive. Even though he was no longer alive, I could still feel and connect to his vibrational energy. If I could feel his vibrational energy, then did that mean that he was still somewhere, very much alive? How could his life be snuffed out while his energy remained so strong in me?

I also wondered how he knew he was going to die, because I was absolutely certain that when he came on Mother's Day, he came to tell me goodbye. I believed then, as I do now, that he knew when he came to see me that it would be the last time we would ever see each other in this way (physically) .

Just the fact that he came to tell me good-bye, coupled with the fact that we'd known each other since we were very young, made me realize what a connection we had, and I wanted to find a way to keep the connection alive. I didn't want the vibration that I could still feel as him to fade away as time progressed.

On Thursday of that same week, my grandfather died. I found out on the way back from his funeral. Not only that, but my grandmother was coming to live with us.

It was a lot to deal with. That is an understatement. Two deaths of those I loved in a week caused me to ponder life and death in ways I never had before.

I didn't have much time to ponder. The very next day, a friend was over doing my mom's and grandma's hair for grandpa's funeral. I went down into the basement of our townhouse to check on the dryer. I went down the thirteen steps, and when I got to the bottom and opened the basement door, flames jumped out at me and over my head.

I turned and raced up the stairs. By the time I made it up to the top of the stairs, the flames were at my heels.

The fire was so fast-burning that I barely had time to yell at everyone to get out and grab the family's poodle. I herded everyone into the backyard, and then realized I needed to call 9-1-1, so I headed back into the house to grab the phone.

This was the 1980s – back when the phones still hung on the walls and had really long cords. It wasn't like today where cell phones and cordless phones are rampant. I grabbed the phone, dialed 9-1-1, and hunkered down low below the smoke.

It's a funny thing – knowing that I needed to stay low in the smoke. The reason I knew was that when I was quite young – maybe two or three years old – I saw something on television talking about what to do in a fire. It made a huge impression on me, and I remembered it all of those years.

Once again, I was in a position to know exactly what to do in an extraordinary situation.

On the floor talking with the 9-1-1 operator, I barely had time to tell them where we were before the smoke became too much and started to choke me. I had to get out of the house.

We stood in the backyard watching our house burn. We lived in New York, and the houses were attached to one another. We had to climb several fences to get out of the yard and to the front street to meet the fire trucks.

My dad wasn't home at the time – and when he returned home, the street was blocked off by fire trucks, ambulances and police cars. Little did he know that when he went to make funeral arrangements for his father, he'd come home and find his home going up in smoke and his entire family in the street watching it.

The house was a total loss. Everything was either burned up, smoke-damaged or water-damaged. We were homeless.

Fortunately, my grandmother still had her apartment, so that is where we all went. For months we lived in a one-bedroom apartment while our home was rebuilt.

That week was a turning point in my life. All of these changes and tragedies happening in such a quick succession shook my world at its very core and left me trying to figure everything out. It was the beginning of my absolute yearning to find something more.

CHAPTER 5

Connecting in a New Way

All of the changes left me reeling. At the same time, I started to become aware that I was somehow still connected to my childhood sweetheart and my grandfather. I could still feel their vibrations.

I needed an outlet.

One of the things that changed in me during that awful week was that I could no longer keep all of the things I was experiencing inside of myself. I was thrust full-force into the world that I kept to myself, and I had to let the secret girl out. It became apparent to me that I needed to pay more attention to my inner world and yearnings. I decided I needed to communicate more openly.

I started to share my thoughts and feelings with the boy I was dating. He didn't handle it well. It was just too much for an eighteen-year-old boy, and he misinterpreted what I was trying to communicate with him. He went to his mother, who was a nurse, and told her he thought I was so devastated that I needed help. But it wasn't help that I needed; I just needed to communicate all of my inner turmoil. My secret girl needed a voice.

It was during this time that I met Craig. With Craig, I felt safe to express myself. I was free to delve into those parts of myself that I so needed to shine a light on. Craig vibrated at the energy level that I needed at that time in my life.

Like me, Craig kept parts of himself locked away, and I believe he felt a level of comfort or maybe curiosity with me, and was ready to express some of those parts with me, too. When we met, it was like a crescendo. Each of us fed off of the other, and we went through years of seeking and growing together in a very short time.

All of the longing, the yearning and the discomfort I had experienced all of my life became apparent after the fire. While I had always suspected it, I now knew that there was more to life than what could be seen.

I entered into a relationship with Craig. At the same time, I entered into a time of intense seeking. I went to psychics, read tarot cards and studied numerology and astrology. In all of these things, I sought to fill up this deep yearning that I was feeling, but nothing ever soothed my soul. I knew that no matter how much information I found, there was more to know, and I needed to know it.

Craig was supportive of my seeking, probably because he was searching, too. By the time I was twenty, I didn't have any more answers – but I had something else. I had a baby on the way.

CHAPTER 6

Being a Mom

When my daughter, God-is, was born, it added an entirely different element to my seeking and finding. God-is was a remarkable gift, and she became the center of my universe. Instinctively I understood that spirit was coming through me for her. I had a responsibility to give her the entire universe. Now I was seeking for two.

God-is came at a time when I was seeking answers in such an intense way, it felt as if she were an answer to one of my questions about what my responsibilities were, what my path was, and how I fit into the universe. My whole life became about making sure that I exposed God-is to as many things as I possibly could.

My daughter was the joy of my life. Someone once said that motherhood is like having your heart running around outside of your body. For me, it was even more than that. While I knew and understood that this little being was a separate soul from me, it was as if her soul fully encompassed mine. There was no separation between my desires for myself and my desires for her.

Motherhood was an amazing fit for me. I believed then – as I do now – that I was born to be a mother. There are plenty of books that talk about motherhood but none that I have read has come close to explaining the intensity of that relationship and the strength of that bond. Everything in my life revolved around God-is. Everything moment of my life, every breath I took, and every experience I had became focused on the one tiny spot in this vast, unending universe that was God-is.

As a mother, I felt – no, I knew – that I always had to be in tune. It was my sacred duty to be in tune with everything so that God-is could be in tune. She needed to know she could rely on me to raise her in a way where the energy was always pure.

This was the beginning of searching in a way I had never searched before. I needed to know – not just for myself, but for God-is. In doing so, I allowed her to experience different vibrations and exposed her to different energies so that she had an emotional and spiritual foundation. I wanted her to have what I had missed all of my childhood – an awareness of her connection to all and the knowledge of where she fit into everything. But first I had to discover that myself. We would find it together.

Chapter 7

Food for My Soul

We began to make a game of it, God-is and I. We would go to the bookstore and peruse the metaphysical section. We would wait to see which book pulled us in. If a book vibrated in a certain way, then that was the book I would pull off of the shelf and read.

The books were all certainly interesting, and they filled my arsenal with information that felt valuable and true – but I still hadn't found the *one* piece of information that would help to click all of the puzzle pieces into place.

One normal day at Barnes and Noble, I was going about my typical routine when a book literally jumped off of the shelf and landed at my feet. I didn't touch it. I didn't knock the shelf. It jumped. It's a good thing I was paying attention.

I'd heard of this happening to others before – books or other information actually jumping out in front of them. Usually it turned out to be just the information they needed, so you can bet I was going to pay attention to this book.

The book was called *Journey of Souls*. It was written by a doctor named Michael Newton. In the book, Dr. Newton talked about regression hypnotherapy and presented case studies of patients he had worked with. According to Dr. Newton, during a normal regression hypnotherapy session one day, he stumbled upon first the past life of his client, and then an account of what existence was like between lives.

This was the information that my spirit had been yearning for all of my life. I knew it the moment I began reading the book. It was like food for my soul – which had been starving for so long.

I devoured the book. I couldn't put it down, and everything inside of it resonated at the very core of my being. At last, I knew, I had found the path I was meant to walk.

I have never believed that when people die, they just end. To me, that makes no sense. It was innately obvious that the moments of this lifetime – birth and death – were merely a transformation our souls went through in the continuum of life in this universe. I never knew how the transformation took place. But I never, ever doubted that there was a transformation. Now, at last, it appeared I had the answers to the soul's journey in my hands.

I quickly read *Journey of Souls* and then moved on to Dr. Newton's second book, *Destiny of Souls*, in which he presented more case files and explained the structure of how our souls lived when not in human form. I was hooked.

CHAPTER 8

What Was I Waiting For?

If I were to read a book in which a chapter began with the words, "fifteen years later," I would wonder what happened in the interim. So what happened for the next fifteen years? Life.

I raised a daughter. I had a career. I had an off and on relationship with Craig. Mostly off.

So there I was, fifteen years later. Boy was I stuck. God-is was seventeen, and she wanted to get out and experience the world in her way, which created tension in our relationship. Craig was gone, and I was grieving the end of a twenty-year sporadic relationship that I'd tried to make work in every way I knew how. I was working at a job in marketing. I was good at my job but it wasn't something that really resonated for me. I didn't enjoy it.

I was living in South Carolina, and I ached to get back home to New York. Several career opportunities presented themselves that would allow me to get closer to home. One, especially, was quite promising, and I was certain I would be picking up and moving to New Jersey to pursue my career there. It wasn't New York, but it was a lot closer to it than South Carolina was. In my mind, it was close enough. I was flown up to New Jersey and had a very positive interview. The company did everything except offer me the job right there on the spot. And then I never heard from them again. Obviously, the universe was blocking me for a reason but I didn't realize or see that. I was just frustrated and I felt like I wasn't getting anywhere in my life. It was like being in a thick fog – where all you can see clearly is that which is in your immediate space.

I don't know if you've ever viewed sunlight through a filter of fog, but if you have, then you will know that a ray of sunlight that pierces a fog is magnified. It is so bright you can't miss it, and you can't ignore it. If you follow it, it will guide you home.

My sister, Tina, provided me with the ray that would serve to carry me home.

I didn't know it at the time, but Tina – who had always known about my "weirdness" – wrote a letter to Michael Newton about me.

In the response she received, she was told that Michael Newton no longer provided life-between-lives (LBL) regressions but she was given the names of three hypnotherapists who had studied his techniques directly with the man. One of those names was Paul Aurand, who lived close to my sister in New York.

Knowing I would be in town for the holidays with the family, my sister made an appointment with Paul for both of us during my visit. It was a Christmas/birthday (my birthday is in early January) present. Next to God-is, it was the single greatest gift that I was ever given.

My sister and Jennifer – who also knows about my "weirdness" – were both going to have hypnotherapy sessions, as well. My sister's was scheduled first, followed by me, and then my cousin.

When my sister went in for her session, Paul told her it was going to be an unusual experience for him. He'd never had three family members before, and it would be interesting to see the soul paths playing out between the three of us.

My sister's session was relatively uneventful. She was looking for specific information, and it didn't come through in the session. Paul explained to her that we can be blocked from receiving information if it isn't time or if we aren't yet ready to receive it. Whatever the reason, Tina didn't really go where she thought she needed things to go.

After her session, however, she told Paul, "When you get to my sister's session, the whole dam is going to break."

When it was time for my session, Paul asked me what my goal was for the session, so that we could try to achieve that through the therapy. I told him that I wanted to understand why I felt so stuck in life, and I wanted to make sense of my burning desire to do more with my life.

By the time I left his office that day, I understood... and I'd never be the same.

Learning from Past Lives

Somewhere, something incredible is waiting to be known.
~Carl Sagan

CHAPTER 9

Buried Memories

What does it feel like to be hypnotized? The experience varies from person to person; however, I can share my perspective from my first time.

I have a very active brain that just doesn't seem to shut down. There are always things going on in my mind – conversations, thoughts, observations, critical analysis. Naturally, going into my first session with Paul, I questioned if hypnosis was possible for me. Fortunately, prior to the session, Paul sent me a recording that talked about hypnotherapy – and past life regression in particular. It also demonstrated the relaxation techniques he would be using in my regression.

Before I went to see Paul, my experience with hypnosis came only from my reading of Michael Newton's books and the "show time" hypnosis I'd seen on television – you know the kind – where the hypnotist pops the subject on the head and the next thing they know they are running around clucking like a chicken.

I didn't really understand what the process would be for induction (guiding me into the hypnotic state). Paul's recording consisted of relaxation techniques and a discussion of how the process of past life regression worked. It was very reassuring to me. It helped for my conscious and critical mind to be able to know the process.

When I got to Paul's office the day of my session, I was immediately at ease. Paul had a wonderful, calming energy that made me feel comfortable.

Prior to the session, Paul and I talked for a while. He asked me what benefits I would like to attain for this Past Life Regression session. He wanted a clear understanding of my perceived benefit and the outcome I hoped for.

I told Paul that I felt stuck, and that my whole life was falling apart. My career – in which I'd always been very aggressive and successful –was now going nowhere. I was unhappy with it. It seemed I was in a holding pattern and couldn't move. I've always been able to work myself out of any situation, and this time, no matter how hard I worked, nothing changed. I no longer knew which way to turn.

I also told Paul that I was curious about past lives, and had been for quite some time. I explained to him my feeling about the sense I had all of my life that there was something more to me and to the world than what I felt as if I knew – or perhaps a better way to explain it would be what I "accepted."

We talked for about 20 minutes. As we talked, I became more and more comfortable. I was really excited about experiencing hypnosis.

Then, Paul explained the process of hypnosis and past life regression to me. He told me that he would count me down, and as I got comfortable, we'd move backwards in time; first to a happy childhood memory, and then deeper – to the womb – after my conception but before my birth. After that, we would regress into a most recent past life.

I relaxed in the chair. I felt an almost instant comfort level with Paul. There was soft music playing that sounded nearly celestial. Paul told me to take deep breaths, relax and just listen to his voice, allowing the tensions to release.

During this process, my conscious mind kept saying, "There's nothing happening." I learned later that this is a very common experience in hypnosis, especially for those who are having their first experience.

In his relaxed, comforting voice, Paul gave me beautiful imagery to focus on, which helped me to relax. Finally he said, "Let's go back to an early childhood happy memory."

At that point, my conscious mind said, "What on earth am I going to remember? What can I think of to tell him – a childhood memory?"

Paul told me to relax and allow the scene to open up. He told me to relax and let it happen.

All of a sudden, this deep emotion opened up in me, and I started crying. I had a deep sense of what felt, at the moment, like sadness.

Paul asked what I was experiencing, and told me to take my time. When I felt ready, I could begin to tell him what I was experiencing. He told me to get a sense of my surroundings.

At this point, my conscious mind was really wondering what was happening. Clearly I was remembering something. Not only was I remembering, but I was also deeply feeling it. My conscious mind was asking how I could be feeling something I didn't remember. I was a bit confused, but also compelled to understand.

As quickly as I had started, I stopped crying. Paul asked what was happening. My response....

"I don't know."

Paul told me to take time and allow the scene to open up. He gave me a few moments to adjust my focus. This is extremely important in hypnotherapy – the ability to tune into your client and know when to give them time and when to interject is paramount.

When I seemed ready, he asked me what I saw.

"I don't see anything."

Again, Paul told me to just relax and try to get a sense of where I was. He gave me permission to bring my awareness to the experience, and suddenly I was able to.

I was obviously in trance. I was beginning to grasp this new space or new found awareness. I remember thinking consciously....WOW. Interestingly, I was also quite AMAZED at my awareness of a whole other part of myself that somehow felt very familiar and always present. More importantly, I felt safe and at ease – not threatened in any way. Oddly, this new awareness was somehow very familiar.

It was like a doorway opened up. Beyond it was great potential and a sense of understanding. I felt a profound sense of curiosity and wonderment. I was truly amazed. It was at this time that my conscious mind stepped aside. Now I decided it was time to focus, let go and allow the experience to happen. I listened to Paul's voice and watched this newfound awareness slowly unfold and take its place at center stage.

I tried to look around. Looking around in this state means focusing internally and waiting to see what images, feelings and visions come forth. It was then that I realized I couldn't see anything. I got a sense that my eyes were covered. Paul asked me to focus and see why my eyes were covered and to sense what was covering them.

Suddenly I realized – there was a scarf around my eyes. It came to me so easily once I learned to focus. I was learning to give way to the process and allow awareness to open up to me.

Paul asked me where I was. It took me a few minutes to respond, and then I told him that it felt like I was in a closet. He asked where the closet was, and why I was in it.

Once again, my response was, "I don't know."

Although it was feeling easier, I was still adjusting to this new experience. Initially, I was focused on learning to feel and accept the awareness, and then learning to allow the information to come through that was specific to the questions he was asking me.

"Yes, you do," Paul told me. "Look and see where you are. Focus on your surroundings. Focus your attention to find out where you are and why you are there."

"The kids put me in the closet." I responded, somehow knowing that innately.

"Who are these kids?" Paul asked. "How old are you?"

And then, just like that, I knew the answer. "I'm three or four," I told Paul. "My cousins put me in the closet."

"Why?" he asked.

"Because they thought I was a baby, and they wanted to be mean. We were playing 'Pin the Tail on the Donkey,' and they put me in the closet and closed the door."

Suddenly the memory was fully formed in my mind. I remembered being heartbroken that they would do that to me. (This is where the initial burst of tears came into play – the sadness I felt in the very beginning.) Now I began to wonder, and I thought to myself consciously, *I thought we were supposed to be going to a HAPPY memory.*

At first, I was afraid in the closet. But then, a feeling of comfort came over me, and I knew there was nothing to be afraid of. A voice inside of me told me to be strong and show them that I wasn't a baby.

I burst out of that closet and yanked the scarf from my eyes. I told them that they might all be afraid of being in the closet but I wasn't, and if they did it to me again, I was going to tell.

From that point forward – until this very day – I have had an almost invisible respect from my cousins.

I started to cry after reliving that memory because it was ultimately a very happy memory. It was wonderful to reconnect with the tremendous sense of accomplishment I experienced in that moment when I told bigger kids that I wasn't going to be pushed around anymore.

Now it was really starting to make sense. This sense of facing my fears and being the youngest and having the courage to do what I sensed even the older kids were afraid of. That feeling of confidence has always been with me from that day on. It was amazing how I'd forgotten or conveniently placed this experience deep in my subconscious but held on to the sense of confidence the experience brought me.

It was at this point in the session where my conscious mind really stepped back in a tangible way. Hypnosis helped to facilitate a memory I hadn't thought about in almost 40 years.

Paul allowed me to spend some time in the memory, and told me to bring those feelings of pride, strength and courage with me into my life now.

I did and it was wonderful. Having that experience really gave me such joy and a certain confidence in this thing called hypnosis. Here I was, remembering a long ago memory consciously forgotten. Now I could see it all so clearly, as if it were just yesterday. All of the emotions, and thoughts tied to that experience were now crystal clear and present.

I was ready to move on, and ever so eager to see what was next. My curiosity and excitement grew, and I was now ready for the next experience.

Paul sensed I was ready and began instructing me to go deeper into relaxation.

He counted: "Three, going deeper....that's it....two... even deeper...now one...relaxing even deeper."

CHAPTER 10

Deeper into the Past

Paul took me deeper to my next stop – to the womb. By this point, my conscious mind was fully relaxed. It was just sitting back and observing the whole process.

When Paul said he'd be taking me to the womb, my conscious mind thought, *Oh – now this is going to be interesting*. I couldn't imagine what I'd remember from that far back, but I was exhilarated from the last experience, so I was ready to go.

Paul gave me a few minutes to settle in, and then he asked me what it was I was sensing, and what my relationship was to my mother.

I was astounded. Everything was clear as a bell, and I had a clear sense of the situation and the vibrations of the situation. My first awareness was that it was cold – because it was very cold in the house. I was aware that my mother was cold.

In my memory, I saw that my mother was living with my great grandmother, who wasn't always terribly nice to my mom. Not only that, but my mother spent a lot of time worrying about my father, who was away in Germany in the Army. I told Paul that sometimes my mother was afraid, but that I helped her by sending her happy thoughts.

This experience, I found, came to me much more easily but it was far more complex. Let me try to explain...the images and feelings were so fluid they easily came forth. In this experience, I had an awareness of myself sitting in Paul's office in the chair. I was also aware of my mother's feelings, and the feelings of those around her. At the same time, I had an awareness of myself as spirit – not in a physical body, but as an existence or a true awareness. I could also sense the presence of others in spirit around me. And then there was the sense of the developing body. Not only that, but I was doing things in this awareness...I was sending my mother "happy thoughts" to keep her comfortable!

This was a whole new awareness and in an odd way, it felt closer to me, closer to the real ME. The one I always knew but had forgotten. The one that was not bound to a body or a thought or any limitations as we know them in the physical linear plane. There are no words to describe it. All I knew was that it felt right and I had such excitement from beginning to remember again.

Paul asked me if it was typical for me to come to my mothers in each of my lives before my birth to take care of them.

"Yes, I do it all of the time," I told him.

Next, Paul asked me where I was in relationship to the developing body.

"Sometimes in and sometimes out," I said.

"What do you do when you're out?" Paul asked me.

"I'm helping."

I went on to explain to Paul that I have jobs to do, and that part of my job is to help.

"There are angels all around that help me to take care of my mom, too," I told him.

These answers were coming to me so flawlessly and fluidly. There was no thinking or hesitation. It was as if this information was there all along, just waiting for me to tap into it. It was from my core – from my source – and it was the purest and most comfortable feeling I'd ever experienced. There was no force, just simply a wonderful flow of information.

Paul asked me to describe the angels, and I told him that some have bodies and some don't. I remember clearly that, in that moment in my session, the angels felt more real to me than anything in my current terrestrial life.

Next, Paul asked me to describe to him my purpose and goals in this life.

"To help," I told him. "I have many jobs to do, but all are connected to helping."

I also told Paul that the angels helped me in this lifetime, and that they were always all around. They came with me when I decided to come back to the physical plane this time.

Paul asked me if the angels said anything to me, and I told him that they tell me to stay in tune and remember, and that they encourage me.

"Tell me how you help," Paul said.

"I don't know. I can't really tell you how. I just know it is my job to help."

"Who have you come to help?" he asked.

"I don't know. I can't tell you how or who. I just know it is my job to help. When I ask the angels they tell me, 'You will see.'"

During this part of the session, it became apparent that I had the ability to communicate with these angels, and inside I began asking them questions. The entities were speaking to me. I couldn't see them but I could hear and feel them.

Paul took me deeper into the experience, asking if there was anything I could tell him about my developing body.

"The angels tell me to pay attention," I said. "I am stronger than the body. I chose this body even though I knew it had limitations. The limitations were to help me learn the lessons I came here to experience. I knew I would have a job to do before I decided to come back to the physical plane."

To say the least, this was NOT expected, but I longed to understand my purpose. I was here right at the core of understanding having been given a clear connection to the source of my questions, and I was exhilarated, amazed, and in awe.

I was getting clear answers about me. It felt right and to some degree, it gave me a sense of satisfaction, but I craved to get closer to a better understanding. I wondered what did "help" mean?... Job? What jobs? And who was it I was to help? What did all of this mean? I was ready to find the answers and Paul sensed I was ready, too.

Next, Paul asked me if there was anything I wanted to know before we went to a past life. I told him no, and he counted me deeper into the past.

Chapter 11

The First Lesson: Let Go

When I let go of what I am, I become what I might be.
~Lao Tsu

Immediately, I started gasping. I was having some kind of a strange reaction and I felt like I couldn't breathe. I also became aware of physical pain in the area of my womb.

I knew immediately what was going on. I had just given birth and died during childbirth. This wasn't something I necessarily saw – it was something I knew intuitively.

I had regressed to a past life, and apparently straight to the death scene in that life.

I was overcome with tremendous sadness because I died and had to leave my child behind. I felt as if I spent an eternity floating in despair because I didn't want to leave the baby. What I felt was a genuine sense of grief.

After a few minutes, Paul asked me if I was alone.

I was so overcome with grief and sorrow I could not focus on anything else. The sense of sadness consumed me so much that it took up my entire awareness. It wasn't until Paul asked me if I was alone that I realized I was not.

"No," I told him. "My guide is here."

At the moment I became aware of HIS presence, I was overwhelmed with a deep feeling of love and patience. I instantly knew I'd known this entity forever, and HE knew every single thing about me. I felt as though HE was connected to every ounce of my being, and HE nourished me with unconditional love. HE emanated a feeling of tremendous love, understanding and pride for me.

My guide took me to a quiet place, where we sat and talked.

I think I'd better back up for a minute here because the concept can be a little difficult to grasp. In the conversation that followed with my guide, it was happening in real time, even though I was in the midst of regression hypnotherapy. That's because, in a hypnotic trance, I was able to move into a state of super consciousness where I was aware not only of the past life and its regression but also of things that were happening in real time. This isn't unheard of in hypnotherapy, and has been documented by many hypnotherapists including Dr. Brian Weiss, author of *Many Lives, Many Masters*.

Think of it this way. It is kind of like when you are having a dream where you are aware that you are dreaming during the dream. You may be aware on many levels during such a dream. Your awareness may be as the person in the dream, the person observing the dream and the person evaluating the dream. In that moment, your awareness exists on many levels and in many timelines. It is merely a matter of where you focus your attention as to what experience you walk away from the dream with. The BIG difference here is that during hypnosis, consciousness is not suspended as it is in the sleep state.

In hypnosis, your awareness is different. You move from the BETA state, which is the "waking state," where reasoning, logic and decision making occurs. This state is sometimes referred to as a linear state. From the BETA state, you move into the ALPHA state or "hypnotic state".

This is where learning, creativity, imagination and meditation take place. This state is not linear, and is very different in the way we experience things consciously.

There are two more states of consciousness: the THETA state or "dream state," which is where it is reported that spiritual awareness takes place, and finally, the DELTA state, where deep sleep happens as a total suspension of consciousness. Therefore, it all is quite easy to keep track of, and the ability to interchange with the perception of each is natural – from the person experiencing the past life, to the person that you are right now, to who you are as a spirit, to the person who is observing. You become hyperaware, and the experience, lessons, and information you gain from the session stem from what your intended goal is in the beginning, as well as your readiness for the experience. Your hypnotherapist guides the focus of your attention.

So there I was, in Paul Aurand's office, talking with my guide. There was tremendous comfort in HIS presence, and HIS words were wise and filled me deeply to my core.

Paul asked me if my guide had a name. Without knowing how I knew, I immediately sensed that my guide's name was ALL, and that we had been together for a very long time. In HIS presence, I could feel HIS deep desire to help and guide me.

At first, ALL talked to me about the life I had just experienced. HE told me that I had to move forward from that experience and let go. HE also told me that the life I'd just left was connected to the life before that – and that all of my lives were connected as experiences for growth. It is that way for everyone, ALL explained. We must learn and move forward in our paths as souls. We all take on a physical body to work things out for ourselves.

It was at that point I recognized that my daughter, the baby I so reluctantly had to leave in my past life, was my daughter in my current life. It was a truly breathtaking experience to recognize someone at a soul level, and to know that we all are connected no matter how much we choose to forget.

ALL told me that I needed to let go of the pain from that life, because only in letting go would I be able to move forward spiritually. The most important part of that life – and of any experience – was to grasp the understanding the experience had created. All experiences have lessons, and all lessons have purpose. HE told me that I needed to let go of the pain and embrace the understanding. It was that understanding, HE explained, that would allow me to move forward. HE said there was no need to hold on to it.

"THE CHILD WAS FINE," HE told me. "SHE CHOSE THE PATH – NOT HAVING A MOTHER – JUST AS YOU CHOSE YOUR PATH IN THAT LIFE OF LEAVING HER AT HER BIRTH. HER LESSON WAS TO LEARN TO GET THROUGH WITHOUT A MOTHER. YOUR LESSON WAS TO UNDERSTAND THAT EVERYTHING WAS DIVINE AND HAD A PURPOSE."

"THERE IS NO LOSS IN THAT EXPERIENCE," ALL told me. "THERE IS ONLY GAIN AS WE BECOME CLOSER TO WHO AND WHAT WE REALLY ARE."

As I began to understand and internalize ALL's words, I was able to allow the pain to ease, calm down and honor the decision that both my daughter and I made in that lifetime.

CHAPTER 12

Lesson Two:
Pay Attention

Tell me to what you pay attention
and I will tell you who you are.
~Jose Ortega y Gasset

The entire conversation with ALL took place internally. It was sort of in my head but, more accurately, in my soul. I was able to keep Paul aware to some degree of what was happening, although this experience was internal. I would tell Paul what we were talking about. It was like being on the telephone with someone and having a conversation, but also having someone in the room with you that cannot hear the person on the other end of the line. In that case, you keep them clued in so that they have an idea of the context of the conversation.

Paul would ask questions, as well, which kept the three-way conversation going. It was awesome. Paul knew something very extraordinary was happening for his client, and so did my guide. Together, they worked to allow me to discover what I needed. It was the kind of self-discovery I'd been searching for all my life. I was finally remembering what I'd always known I had forgotten.

"Is your guide always the same one?" Paul asked me. "Is HE always with you?"

"Yes. HE has been with me many, many, many lives – but HE is many, HE says. I'm not sure what that means but I feel HE is a compilation of many different experiences and guides. The essence of HIM has always been with me."

"What does HE look like?" Paul wanted to know.

"HE presents HIMSELF to me as male because that is my preference," I told him. "HE is a beautiful pure white bright energy in a cloak."

"Look at yourself," Paul instructed. "What do you look like?"

I brought my awareness to myself and saw that I was a golden ball of loving energy. The light and energy that emanated from me was warm and wonderful.

ALL told me that I'd done well, and HE was extremely proud of me. It was at this point that Paul directed questions to ALL, while I served as a bridge between the two. Paul's questions were aloud, and I relayed ALL's answers. It was apparent that I became the conduit – the vehicle – in this conversation, much like a telephone between two people. I gladly embraced this space and learned a great deal from the exchange.

"Why is Lisa stuck?" Paul asked ALL through me.

According to ALL, the reasons that I was stuck in my life at this time were Divine. HE said I was stuck because it was time to get my attention. It was time for me to realize what I had come into this life to accomplish. It was for that reason that my relationships, my job and what seemed like everything else in my life was not moving and was painful and frustrating for me. Getting stuck was the only way to get me to focus inward and discover why I was here, in this life. It was time to begin to remember.

Now that I had come to this understanding of my divine holding, ALL began to talk to me about letting go of the pain and finding the gift in this life, accepting it and using it to serve the purpose that I was here to fulfill.

ALL began to describe to me the kind of entity that I am and the kind of soul I have been throughout my incarnations. HE said my lives had always been about work. HE told me that we all choose the kind of lives we will live before we incarnate. We choose the lessons to be learned, much like we choose courses when going to college. HE said that I always choose painful, difficult, hard lives because for me, it is in those lives where the lessons are greatest and the potential for growth is rich and fertile.

The hardest lives, ALL told me, are those that propel you to the greatest growth. I chose those lives because I aspire to be a guide, as ALL is. According to ALL, it is my passion, my job and my mission to shed light and pave the way for others.

In hearing this, I could not hold back the tears. It all made sense. It felt so right and resonated with what I knew it to be true with every ounce of my being. I felt it, I knew, and I was at home.

Finally the internal pulling inside me all made sense. It was to make sure when it was time I would remember. It was time to wake up to my true nature, and to help others do the same. My purpose was unfolding, and the feelings of honor and responsibility overwhelmed me with joy. The profound gratitude and love I felt for ALL overcame me. I felt that HE has guided me through what could considered as centuries, millions of lifetimes, never ever giving up on me. HE has always had my highest good at heart. How blessed I felt, and how completely I wanted to do the same for others.

ALL continued. "BECAUSE OF YOUR LOVE OF HELPING SOULS," HE said, "YOU HAVE ALWAYS COME BACK EACH TIME ON EARTH TO A MISERABLE, DIFFICULT LIFE SO THAT YOU COULD LEARN MORE AND MORE."

"THIS LIFE," HE said, "YOU CHOSE A LITTLE DIFFERENTLY. IT WILL BE DIFFERENT BECAUSE YOU CHOSE THIS TIME TO LEARN WITHOUT IT BEING SO PAINFUL."

The reason I made this choice for this life, ALL told me, is that I was nearing the end of my incarnations.

I asked ALL about a person whom I'd had an instant connection with since we were 11. Over the years, we've been in and out of each other's lives. I was always curious about him. No matter how many months or years we were apart, whenever life would bring us together, it was as if no time at all had passed. There was truly a special connection, and I had a burning desire to find out why.

ALL said, "YOU HAVE A STRONG SOUL BOND."

HE told me that we have been together in many, many lives helping each other. HE told me I decided in most of my lives not to be connected to a soul mate. HE said I felt that connection would be distracting to what I needed to do. ALL told me I sacrificed this side of myself for the sake of the learning, and for what I could do for the whole (everyone).

"IN THIS LIFE, HOWEVER," HE said, "YOU WILL HAVE THE OPPORTUNITY TO CHOOSE. YOU WILL ALLOW YOURSELF TO HAVE TO OPPORTUNITY TO CHOOSE TO BE CONNECTED."

ALL went on to tell me that the one thing I allowed myself in most of my lifetimes was a strong support system. Because my lives have been so difficult, I chose the same supporters to help me get through. But I never chose to connect to a soul mate. I was excited, finally a connection. What a wonderful thing to learn.

CHAPTER 13

A Broader Perspective

As ALL was speaking, I knew deep at my core that everything was true. HIS words were the answer to my entire life. It was the answer I had been seeking since I was a very little girl.

Discovering these things about myself, including my roles and responsibilities in this lifetime, caused everything to make sense. Suddenly, I had a broader understanding that gave me a sense of peace about my life and showed me why I was here. It was an understanding I had never felt before.

There was a lot of conversation about forgiveness and letting go. There was review of specific occurrences in my life, and the reasons and purpose behind these things. I was shown how anger, blame and holding onto to pain was holding me back from my life's purpose. Instead of blaming, ALL urged me to look for the understanding from the experiences. HE told me to look beyond the eyes and use my heart. HE gave me the knowledge that I was larger than the experiences. They were just tools to help me move forward.

My father used to tell me, "It's the pain and discomfort that you find in life that usually awakens you, and allows you to step up to the next level."

This seemed remarkably valid in light of the conversation I was having with my guide. Once again, my father's teachings had served and nurtured me in my path to my true self.

The conversation with ALL was extremely in-depth, as one might expect a conversation with one's guide to be. We talked about not resisting change, soul choices and why I had chosen the limited body I have for this lifetime. It turns out that I chose to be Lisa Watts because this body had the mental capacity to easily accept change, rather than fight it.

The mind of this current body I occupied, ALL told me, had the capability of allowing a strong connection; a strong connection to spirit and to the other side, which would be imperative to the tasks that were to come.

I was curious about other souls – family members and friends that had passed on. So I asked ALL if I could see some of the other members of my soul group who had passed on.

"NO," HE said, not unkindly. "THAT IS NOT THE PURPOSE OF THIS EXPERIENCE. THE PURPOSE IS TO HELP YOU. AT THIS TIME, IT ISN'T ABOUT CONNECTING TO THOSE WHO HAVE GONE BEFORE YOU," HE SAID. "THIS EXPERIENCE IS TO CONNECT YOU TO WHO YOU REALLY ARE, AND FOR YOU TO BEGIN TO ACCEPT AND UNDERSTAND THAT CONNECTION AND YOUR CHOSEN PURPOSE."

HE told me that as I moved forward, I would learn more and more about myself, and things would begin to unfold naturally. I would need time to digest all of this information in my conscious mind. ALL told me that eventually my conscious mind would begin to expand to grasp and accept this experience and the information given. HE said I would because it was why I was here, in this life.

HE went on to explain that as I moved forward, I would be able to create bridges and roads that would give people the opportunity to be able to find their way as I have found mine.

ALL began to direct HIS statements to Paul. HE told Paul that HE would have to help me understand, in my fully conscious state, that what I was experiencing was absolutely real and true. HE told me that as time went by, things would start to open up for me, and my feeling of stagnation would start to give way to newness. HE also said that Paul and I would continue to work together in some capacity.

After about three hours – which went by in an instant to me – Paul asked if it would be a good time to end. I said yes and I felt ALL began to pull HIS energy back. ALL's energy was one of regality and nobility. HE was loving and pure and extremely strong in presence. I knew then, as HE pulled HIS energy back, that I would never ever in this life forget HE was merely a thought away.

Paul brought me out of the trance, and we sat and talked about the experience.

My first response was, "WOW – I didn't expect that to happen."

I was profoundly moved by my first experience with past life regression hypnotherapy. It was so much more than I had ever expected. At the same time, the wheels were turning in my conscious mind.

Like anyone would be, my immediate feelings were equal parts wonder and skepticism. I had the same doubts, as anyone else would have had, given what I had just experienced. At the same time, I had such a desire all of my life, it felt as if everything had suddenly crystallized and I finally understood my life. I had a sense of release from the inner pulling as I'd never had before, and I finally understood that strong stirring feeling that there was something more to life.

No matter what my conscious mind was doing, somewhere inside of me I knew that what had happened was real and true. I intuitively knew the divineness of my experience.

My conscious mind was going crazy trying to make logical of what had happened. At the same time, I knew it was just a ramification of not being able to consciously grasp such a profound experience.

As ALL told to me, over time my consciousness fell more in line. I spent a lot of time reflecting and re-examining the situations in my life. I focused more internally, and began to pay more attention to the voice inside, my feelings, and the bigger picture of the happenings around me.

Slowly, after that first session, my life began to move. It didn't happen right away, which bummed me out since I was looking for an instantaneous fix. But this was a process – one that would be long lasting and profound.

I held on to the feelings from that time spent with my guide. In time, things began to unfold. As they did, I was able to become more and more trusting about the path that my life was destined to follow.

During the course of our session, ALL told me that my mind was always full of chatter. So much so that often my focus was impaired. The chatter and things that I held in my conscious mind were obstructing my ability to access my gifts.

ALL told me I have the gift of connection, and Paul asked how I could connect to ALL when I was not in hypnosis.

ALL made a simple but profound statement. "ALL SHE HAS TO DO IS FOCUS."

As one whose mind is always doing multiple things, this simple statement was an extremely moving one for me.

We all have the ability to choose where we place our awareness each and every moment. We have the ability to choose our thoughts, and to give way to those inner thoughts that guide us in all we do. You are no different than I am in this respect – it is a matter of learning to focus our attention.

It took me some time, but eventually I learned to be more adept at that one simple but profound task. I learned to focus and pay attention.

And my life opened up. Finally... MOVEMENT!

CHAPTER 14

Movement

My first session with Paul was in January, 2005. It took me eighteen months to process the information I had received and be ready to move forward.

During my first session, I received a lot of very deep information. It was as if I opened a new door that I never knew existed. At the same time, I always knew that it was there. It was the door behind which my secret girl was hidden most of my life. Once the door opened, I felt like I'd been exposed to a wondrous place where the connection I sought for my entire life existed. In that first session with Paul, I received a glimpse of who I truly was. It was amazing that such a place existed in me – as it exists inside of everyone – where I could connect to who and what I really was.

I'm not for a moment suggesting that acceptance came easily. It didn't. I struggled with that information for eighteen months. I spent the time well – wrapping my active and critical brain around what I'd learned, and allowing the information I'd learned in the experience to sink in. Internally, I accepted the experience as truth almost immediately. But it took some time for my brain to catch up with my soul and my gut.

There's a divide in me – as there is a division in so many of us. My secret girl has always known what she knows. There was never a problem convincing her. My critical mind, however, was another story entirely. That part became enmeshed in a fight for its very survival. To this point, my critical brain had always run the show. Now, it was losing dominance and the secret girl was moving to the forefront. And that girl was challenging the self-definition my critical brain had been building for nearly four decades.

My critical brain wanted proof – and lots of it – while the secret girl was really excited to finally receive such validation and acknowledgement. She was ready to go, just waiting for the rest of me to catch up.

It turned out to be a very slow and arduous process. If I expected immediate movement as a result of my profound insights, then I was bound to be disappointed. I did, and I was. I thought that my stifled feelings would immediately be removed. It didn't work that way. Instead, it was a process. Each and every moment for eighteen months, I was learning, absorbing, and reframing my world-view. Looking back now, it has a feeling of the fable, *The Tortoise and the Hare*. I was the tortoise, when I expected to be the hare.

Slow and steady ruled the day. Little by little, my life started to open up, and my circumstances began to change. I have a hunch that I slowed down the process quite a bit because of the dichotomy inside of me. Internally, I had amazing spiritual insight. Externally, however, I was linear and concrete. It took a while for this conflict to resolve. My mind had to challenge me to rise to the occasion.

At first, I didn't really share with others what had happened during my session with Paul. I needed to work it out internally, occasionally sharing something with someone.

I listened to the recording of the session over and over again. I'd think, then listen. Think some more, and then listen again.

One of the most difficult things to wrap my mind around was the question we all ask ourselves at some point. Why me? Why on earth would I be chosen for all of this? And then, I realized it didn't matter. My ego was asking that question. My spirit knew the whys and hows, if only I would pay attention to it.

I longed for the change that ALL had promised was coming. I felt like I was still trapped in a divine prison. I knew I was there to learn to pay attention, and ultimately paying attention was what allowed my conscious mind to begin to trust.

I sat back and watched things as they unfolded. Slowly, my life began to move forward. As the months went by, I noticed changes. Newness. Not a lot, but enough to see that things were, indeed, moving forward. I got a new job. My daughter, who had been estranged from me, found her way back to me and back to herself.

Gradually, I felt differently, saw things differently, and began to pay more attention. I was learning to balance the secret girl with my critical mind. And it was a true balance. I didn't let the inside take over but at the same time, my critical brain wasn't so much in control anymore, either.

After about eighteen months, I felt like I'd grown but I didn't feel like I was yet where I needed to be. I decided that I needed to have another past life regression. I didn't know what I'd get, and I didn't know what to expect. I just knew that it was time. I had finally fully embraced the first experience, and I was ready for more.

CHAPTER 15

Ready for More

Paul was very accommodating. Seeing him again was like coming home. Whatever the connection we'd previously had was still there.

We discussed some of the changes that had occurred in my life. Paul asked how I was feeling, and I told him I felt I was on the cusp of breaking into something new now that I'd made it through the stuff that was keeping me stuck. I was following my spirit for the first time in my life, and I felt as if I was on the verge of something, and I was ready to figure out what it was. I eagerly anticipated what I would discover in this new adventure.

When I made the second appointment with Paul, he asked that I write ten questions about things that I felt I wanted to get answers to. He told me it was my time and my opportunity for learning, so I could ask about anything – about my past, present, future, relationships – it was up to me.

I arrived at Paul's office with about a dozen questions in hand. They ranged from the feeling of anticipation I was experiencing to a question about my relationships with others.

Because I prepared questions, I understood that the session would be a Q&A but I didn't know how on earth I would receive the answers. Would they be in the form of a memory or something else altogether? I was excited that I might get an answer to even one or two of the questions I had.

It turned out that I was really easy to induce this time. Paul counted me down using the same relaxation techniques he'd done before, and I was immediately in a death scene. This time, I didn't have to travel back through my own childhood or into the womb. Instead, as soon as he counted, there I was. Dying. Again.

CHAPTER 16

Lesson Three: Every Life Has a Divine Purpose

Whatsoever that be within us that feels, thinks,
desires, and animates, is something celestial,
divine, and, consequently, imperishable.
~Aristotle

First came the shortness of breath. Then there was a tightening sensation in my chest. And before I had a chance to figure out who, what or where I was, I went into the place where I'd spoken last time with ALL. I was in a life between lives, and I could feel the awareness entering me as I struggled to get my bearings.

This is normal – struggling to get your bearings. It happens to people who have had a near-death experience. It is a little disorienting to transition from one dimension to another, and it takes a few moments to move into the new state of being that exists in a different dimension.

"What's happening?" Paul asked.

"I've moved into some place."

"Get a sense around you and tell me what's going on," Paul instructed me gently.

I looked around me, and noticed that things were becoming clear. I had just transitioned over from life to death. I had a sense of knowing that this transition was much easier than transitions I'd experienced when leaving other bodies.

Paul told me to notice where I was in relation to my old body.

"I'm at HOME," I told him. "The body is gone."

"Tell me what it's like at HOME," Paul said.

"It's quiet."

As Paul instructed me to take my time and look around, I knew that I'd had a mild heart attack, but that I was tired and ready to go HOME, so I did. I had been a Caucasian male in my mid to late 50s.

"Are you alone?" Paul asked me.

"Yes. I am alone now."

"What is happening in this quiet place?" Paul wanted to know.

"I sit, I think, and I rest."

"What do you think about?"

"The next task," I told him.

Paul asked me what my next task was going to be like.

"My next task is now," I started to tell Paul, meaning that my next task was this life that I currently live, as Lisa Watts. And then, suddenly ALL was there. HE has a very powerful and regal essence about HIM. HE's forceful – not timid, but wise and pristine. As ALL stepped in, the me I know as Melissa stepped aside and became the observer.

"GOOD. VERY GOOD," ALL said. "SHE'S DONE WELL. IT IS I, ALL. I AM HERE WITH HER. SHE IS DOING WELL AS ALWAYS."

A good therapist never assumes, and Paul is a very good therapist. "Are YOU her guide?" he asked.

"YES, I AM."

"How may we call YOU?" Paul asked.

"AND YOU MAY CALL ME ALL."

And then, to my surprise HE said, "SHE HAS QUESTIONS, YES? I AM READY."

This really caught me by surprise. Here was ALL, coming to sit and have a conversation, like a teacher with a student. HE was present, aware and focused. HE knew that I had questions, and HE came to answer them.

Paul began to read from my list of questions. "She feels like she is on the verge or edge of a new direction. She is wondering what's coming and about the details that YOU can offer her."

"YES. I HAVE BEEN LETTING HER KNOW SHE HAS BEEN MOVING INTO NEWNESS."

That was all HE said. So much for details.

Paul asked my next question. "There seems to be a theme with relationships with her. Can YOU help her with that and some of the individuals in question? Is there something regarding her relationships in general? Can YOU expand on that?"

The theme to my relationships has been this: I haven't had any that were lasting or sustainable. I wanted to know why I had chosen that.

"SHE HAS CHOSEN TO LEARN AND UNDERSTAND INTIMACY," ALL answered. "SHE HAS WORKED SO HARD AND GAINED KNOWLEDGE AND HAS LACKED INTIMACY. THIS IS NOT SOMETHING SHE SHOULD WORRY ABOUT. SHE HAS GAINED INTIMACY. SHE HAS GAINED INTIMACY WITH OTHERS AND NOW IT IS TIME FOR HER TO RECEIVE THAT BACK. SHE LONGS FOR THIS BECAUSE IT IS PART OF HER PLAN. GIVING AND TAKING IS THE BALANCE OF LIFE. HER HEART HAS BEEN HEAVY AND NOW WILL BE LIFTED."

ALL went on to talk about soul connections, contracts, bonds, purposes, recognition and patience. HE told me of my decision to not be connected so that I could do my work.

We come here through contract. Each of us has promises and purposes we have set forth for ourselves. My unique purpose was focused on helping others. But I'd never realized that I was gaining intimacy, and ALL showed me that I was.

The soul that ALL described to me, my "true self," felt like an imprint of who I was in my life today when it came to my career. That person and that soul were very focused and deliberate. In my career, doing a good job, doing it well and contributing to the team were my number one goals.

CHAPTER 17

Lesson Four: Be Still and Listen

*Listen to your intuition. It will tell you
everything you need to know.*
~Anthony J. D'Angelo

When ALL had completed HIS answer, Paul asked my next question. "She is wondering what is happening with the state of the world."

"THE WORLD IS IN A FLUX," ALL told us. "THE COLLECTIVE CONSCIOUSNESS IS ON THE BRINK OF CHANGING. THERE IS A CERTAIN UNCERTAINTY. SHE SENSES THAT. SHE IS SENSITIVE. SHE PICKS UP MORE THAN SHE PAYS ATTENTION TO. I MUST BE VERY LOUD WITH HER. SHE FILLS HER MIND WITH TOO MANY THINGS OF THE WORLD. SHE'S GOTTEN BETTER. IT'S TIME TO ACCESS HER GIFTS IN THIS LIFE."

Next Paul asked, "Getting more clarity about her purpose and the purpose of her family in this life is important to her. Can YOU explain or help?"

"HER FAMILY IS UNIQUE. THEY ALL HAVE A CONNECTION. THE FAMILY HAS BEEN GIFTED AND HAS RESPONSIBILITY TO SHED LIGHT IN THE WORLD. EACH AND

EVERY IMMEDIATE FAMILY MEMBER HAS A PLAN AND A CERTAIN SET OF RESPONSIBILITIES THAT THEY MUST ADHERE TO. IT IS THEIR DESTINY TO SHOW LIGHT."

"What positive changes can she expect in the near future with family, career, growth and relationships?" Paul asked.

"SHE MUST WAIT AND SEE. BUT ALL GOOD." ALL wasn't very forthcoming with that one, but my trust level with ALL at this point was strong. What I've learned is that guides will block anything that will get in the way of the learning of the individual. So I'd just have to wait and see.

"Is there anything she needs to be focusing on right now?" Paul asked.

"YES. SHE MUST LEARN TO BE AND LISTEN. THINGS WILL BEGIN TO COME FASTER AND SMOOTHER TO HER, SO SHE MUST LEARN TO BE STILL AND LISTEN. THINGS ARE CHANGING IN HER WORLD, AND THE DIRECTIONS WILL COME PURELY FROM LISTENING INTERNALLY, NOT KNOWING. LISTEN... SHE KNOWS."

It was interesting because although Paul was interviewing ALL and talking to both of us, ALL was sending me vibrations that gave me a deeper insight than what Paul was hearing. When HE said "Be" and "Listen," I felt the energy. At the end, when HE said, "SHE KNOWS," I felt a vibration of a nudge. When ALL did that, HE opened up my awareness, and I DID know.

Next, Paul asked about different people in my life with whom I had a strong soul bond. We went through a list of people I had supplied.

ALL explained different things about the various connections in my life, and then said, "LISA'S ROLE IN MANY LIVES WAS TO GIVE COMFORT TO THE WEARY, TO FIGHT FOR THE WEAK AND TO STAND STRONG. SHE HAS MADE MANY ALLIANCES IN HER MANY, MANY LIVES, AND SOULS SOMETIMES STOP BY JUST TO THANK HER."

Paul asked if there were any souls in my current life who had stopped by for that reason.

"YES," ALL answered. "THERE ARE MANY. SHE IS WELL-REVERED HERE. HER DETERMINATION TO LEARN IS QUITE ENDEARING."

I started to cry. It was very emotional for me to hear and feel what I was feeling from ALL. The tears were short-lived but they came from the feeling of ultimate acceptance and pride that one might have from a parent. It was deeper than that but it is the closest I can come to a description. It was all very overwhelmingly beautiful and touching.

"Is she aware of that?" Paul asked.

"YES. SHE SENSES IT BUT SHE DOESN'T FOCUS ON IT."

Now ALL began to discuss contracts and purposes. He talked about children choosing parents for the growth of a soul. He explained that none of it is bad – it is all experience that is necessary for the soul's growth.

"From my perspective," Paul said when ALL was done, "She has a very wonderful ability to connect with YOU as a guide and to bring information through. Is this something she'll be able to do for the benefit of others?"

ALL's response was loudly thunderous. "OH, YES."

"Can YOU help me understand this more clearly?" Paul asked.

"YES. SHE HAS KNOWN FROM A VERY YOUNG AGE IN THIS LIFE THAT THIS LIFE IS NOT HER OWN BUT THIS LIFE WAS CHOSEN TO BE ABLE TO HELP OTHERS. SHE HAS BEEN GIVEN THE ABILITY TO CONNECT. NOT JUST TO CONNECT HERE BUT TO CONNECT TO THE SOULS AND HEARTS OF MANY. AS WE MOVE FORWARD IN THIS LIFE, SHE WILL BEGIN TO TEACH. AND SHE WILL BEGIN TO HEAL. AND SHE WILL BEGIN TO SHOW THE LIGHT TO PEOPLE ALL OVER THE WORLD. THE CONSCIOUS CONNECTION SHE HAS IN THIS WORLD IS A TRUE BRIDGE TO HERE. THE COLLECTIVE CONSCIOUSNESS IS BEGINNING TO SWITCH AND PEOPLE WILL BE LOOKING FOR

BRIDGES AND ROADS THAT WILL LEAD THEM TO LIGHT. THIS IS WHERE SHE WILL COME IN."

"Is there anything else YOU'd like to convey or communicate to her?" Paul asked.

"THERE ARE ONLY BUT A FEW WEEKS LEFT IN THE CURRENT LIFESTYLE SHE LEADS NOW. SHE MUST START TO BEGIN TO GO WITHIN AND STAY WITHIN BECAUSE SHE WILL BEGIN TO RECEIVE MESSAGES FROM US HERE. THE MOVEMENTS WILL BE SWIFT AND QUIET, AND SHE WILL KNOW. THINGS ARE CHANGING AS WE SPEAK."

Up until this point, most of the conversation had been a Q&A with Paul and ALL, but now I had a question. I started to wonder about the connection I had with ALL and relating it to the last experience I had with HIM.

"SHE IS WONDERING ABOUT OUR CONNECTION," ALL told Paul. "SHE IS TRYING TO FIGURE OUT WHY THIS TIME IS DIFFERENT THAN THE LAST. SHE IS WONDERING WHY THE PROCESS OF COUNTING, GOING THROUGH CHILDHOOD, MOVING THROUGH THE WOMB, THROUGH A PAST LIFE AND COMING HERE – SHE IS WONDERING WHY SHE DIDN'T HAVE TO GO THROUGH THAT.

"IT IS BECAUSE SHE HAS GROWN. SHE HAS BECOME MORE AWARE IN HER UNAWARENESS THAT SHE IS NOW MORE CONNECTED THAN SHE HAS EVER BEEN. THAT IT IS JUST A MATTER OF FOCUS. THERE IS NO NEED FOR ALL OF THE STEPS PRIOR. IT WAS JUST A MATTER OF SHIFTING FOCUS FOR HER."

"Is there a way she can do this on her own?" Paul asked.

"THIS IS QUITE NATURAL TO HER, WHICH IS WHY HER MIND IS TRYING TO PUT IT ALL TOGETHER. IT IS NOT SOMETHING THAT WILL BE SEPARATE FROM WHAT SHE IS. IT IS WHO SHE IS."

"Should she write down or record her experiences, messages or guidance she gets from you?"

"WHAT IS MOST PRACTICAL NOW IS THAT SHE MUST WRITE. ONCE THE EXPERIENCE HAS BEEN HAD, THE MIND –

WHICH IS WHY SHE CHOSE THIS MIND — IS CAPABLE OF HOLDING ALL OF THIS INFORMATION UNTIL IT IS WRITTEN."

I thought maybe I'd have to go home and journal. But typically I don't – this would be unusual for me. Instead, I keep everything in my head. That is where the information has stayed until right now, when I am ready to write it.

"Are there any other messages that YOU have?" Paul asked. "Or, is there a message for me?"

"YES. WHICH IS WHY WE CHOSE YOU. YOU AND SHE IN TIME WILL WORK TOGETHER. YOU AND SHE WILL HELP PEOPLE. NOT NOW, BUT IN TIME. THERE IS A CONNECTION. THERE IS A SENSE OF EASE. AND THERE IS AN AUTOMATIC SENSE OF TRUST BETWEEN THE TWO OF YOU. THAT RELATIONSHIP WILL BE MOVED IN THE DIRECTION TO HELP. YOU ARE CURRENTLY NOW PREPARING FOR WHAT IS TO COME. YOU ARE LAYING THE SEEDS FOR THE NEW ORDER. CONSCIOUSNESS IS SHIFTING, AND PEOPLE WILL BE IN NEED AS PEOPLE WERE IN NEED FOR DOCTORS YEARS AGO. YOU AND SHE AND OTHERS WILL BE THE NEW DOCTORS. THE TIME IS AT HAND. COLLECTIVE CONSCIOUSNESS IS SHIFTING, AND YOU HAVE KNOWN THIS. YOUR PAST FEW YEARS OF EXPERIENCE HAVE TOLD YOU THAT SOMETHING IS HAPPENING AND SOMETHING IS CHANGING AND THAT WE ARE HERE TO HELP TO GROW, TO SEE, TO FORGIVE AND TO COMPLETE OUR PLAN. YOU HAVE GROWN MUCH SINCE OUR LAST TIME TOGETHER, AND YOU, ALSO, HAVE DONE WELL. YOU HAVE CHOSEN YOUR PATH AND THE DOORS FOR YOU ARE OPENING. YOU WILL CONTINUE TO GROW AND DO WELL. WE HERE ARE PLEASED. YOU ARE ONE OF THE FEW THAT HAS MADE A COMMITMENT TO INTEGRITY. INTEGRITY OF THE SOUL."

As I listened to ALL, I was wondering if Paul agreed.

ALL laughed. "SHE IS WONDERING IF YOU AGREE?"

"Yes," Paul said. "Very much so."

I was amazed. I was humbled. I felt very blessed. And, I felt very serious about the job that I had to do. I was serious about figuring it out. I still didn't have a clue – I needed to process the information.

"Lisa, is there anything else that you would like to know?" Paul asked me.

"Yes," I said. I was wondering why it is so dark where we are.

"IT IS BECAUSE YOU FILL YOUR MIND SO MUCH ALL OF THE TIME THAT WHEN YOU COME TO YOURSELF, YOU ASK FOR NOTHING. YOU WANT A CLEAN SLATE SO YOU CAN GET WHAT YOU NEED WITHOUT A LOT OF THE DISTRACTIONS."

That made sense to me. I also asked ALL about the rarified upper echelon people of the world – the haves whose lives appear to be so carefree, those in power, and in governments.

"THERE ARE MANY WHO SEEM TO BE ON TOP IN THIS MAN-MADE WORLD. BUT, IN TRUTH, MANY THAT ARE ON TOP ARE THE ONES HAVING THE HARDEST TIME IN LIFE. THEIR JOURNEYS ARE DIFFICULT AND THEIR KARMA IS HIGH. THINGS IN LIFE ARE NOT – ARE NOT – WHAT THEY APPEAR TO BE. THIS IS IN REFERENCE TO THE POSITIONS OF THE WORLD, POSITIONS IN A COMPANY AND POSITIONS IN A RELATIONSHIP. LISA'S COMFORT LEVEL IS GROWING. HER QUESTIONS OF REAL OR NOT REAL, TRUTH OR NOT TRUTH ARE OPENING UP TO HER. SHE IS OPENING UP TO ACCEPTANCE, AND WILL BE ABLE TO DISCERN MUCH IN TIME."

"I will take time with her when this session is complete to help her gain a deeper understanding and a cognitive awareness of what has transpired," Paul said.

"YES."

"Can YOU help her hold on to the truth of what has transpired here, as well?"

"YES."

"Is there more to be communicated? Is this an appropriate place to conclude?" Paul asked.

"THERE IS ONE LAST THING. SHE WILL FIND HERSELF BEING THE CONNECTION OR THE GLUE TO MANY THINGS THAT WILL TRANSPIRE. WE WANT HER TO UNDERSTAND, AND THAT IS HER RIGHTFUL PLACE. THIS IS WHERE SHE SHOULD BE, AND THAT IS WHERE SHE MUST BE. SHE WILL HOLD THINGS TOGETHER, AND SHE WILL BE THE STRENGTH FOR MANY. SHE WILL HAVE EVERYTHING SHE NEEDS TO COMPLETE THE TASK. THERE SHOULD BE NO ROOM TO WORRY. THERE IS NO ROOM TO WORRY. BECAUSE WE NEED ALL OF HER TO BE FOCUSED ON HER TASK AT HAND WITH GREAT CONFIDENCE. MOVE FORWARD WITH A LIGHT HEART AND CLEAR UNDERSTANDING THAT THIS IS HER DESTINY TO BE IN THAT POSITION."

"Thank YOU," Paul said.

"YES." And with that, ALL began to draw his energy back.

Paul counted me up and brought me to awareness. It was my last in-office session with Paul.

CHAPTER 18

Onward

I was blown away. My session with Paul and ALL took me to places I never thought I'd go. Paul and I discussed it. As ALL had requested, he took a moment to attune to my cognitive brain to let it know that this was all real. It wasn't a game and it wasn't a joke.

My main thought as I left Paul's office was, "What... just... happened?"

Now, I will admit that I was more comfortable than the last time I'd been regressed but now I felt the weight of the responsibility of the gift I've been given.

I also realized, perhaps for the first time in my life, that nothing in my life was an accident. Everything had been so obviously planned. I realized that ALL had intentionally not shared all of this with me the first time, because I wasn't ready for the knowledge.

While I was ready for the knowledge this time, it was still a process. I didn't know what I was going to do. I didn't know how I was going to do it. I just knew that I had to do something.

I needed time to reflect.

ALL told me that things would come faster and smoother – and they did. Not right away, but eventually. I always expect things to be instantaneous, and that isn't always the case. Now, several months after the fact, things did come more quickly and smoothly. But then, every experience that I had that bore out what ALL told me was a tightening of the trust and the bond. Every single thing I moved through went more quickly because I was less dense this time. I can clearly see now that my vibration level had raised. I was moving into acceptance of who I was and what I was here to do.

After I left Paul's office for the second time, things really started to happen quickly for me. Relationships became clearer. It was as if I were going back to the deep sense of awareness I had as a baby – when I was new to this life and this body, and I remembered who I was and where I'd come from. We don't really realize what we take on as we grow up – the thought patterns and beliefs of society, our family – these things all serve to take us away from who we really are.

In the months that followed, I began to understand that I was more than who I thought I was. The self I always referred to as Melissa Watts I understood was a part of me, the past life regression experience taught me that the real me, the spirit, the soul was so much more.

CHAPTER 19

Sedona

For a few months, I did a lot of reading and spent time thinking about all that I'd experienced. In October, I decided to take a class on the development of psychic awareness at the Sedona Sacred Light Institute. It was a certification for the awakening of medical intuitive and psychic skills.

While this didn't feel like my true calling, it was definitely a valuable experience. It was great for me to be in an environment with people who had abilities. It was a safe space for things that I was starting to feel and experience to come out.

I was there for a week, and during that time, things were starting to come up. I was able to be who I was – to be fully immersed in my secret girl rather than hiding it. The people in Sedona began to notice, but I didn't feel uncomfortable like I would have in the "real" world.

I knew, even while I was there, that Sedona was a stepping stone to my ultimate destination. But it did help me to build even more trust – by immersing myself in an environment where there were people who were kind of like me.

It was a wonderful experience to be acknowledged by people who live and think this way all of the time. It was a place where I could let it all out full force. It was wonderful.

While I thrived in this environment, I also knew that it was what I was going to be doing in the future but not exactly this way. We did a lot of work with feeling energies and tapping into vibrations. I don't particularly think of myself as psychic, or have a desire to have others call me that. I think that more than anything, I am connected, and that is how I can pick up energies.

When I returned home from Sedona in November, I knew I needed more experiences to draw me to whatever it was I was being called to do. I just didn't know what experiences I needed. But that's the way of it with me. I never really know what I am supposed to do until it comes along. Until then, I just live and trust. I have to be present.

At first this was scary. I'm pretty linear, and I needed to allow time for my trust to outgrow my fear. It has, and now I know that I am guided.

CHAPTER 20

Finding My Purpose

It was November, and I had a new job. The stresses in my personal life had given way. Life was moving, and I didn't know where it was going to go. But I did know that things were changing.

I'd never really considered hypnotherapy as a career for myself. I thought a lot about the possibilities of hypnotherapy in the context of what it had done for me, and I was impressed with the potential to help others. But I really didn't think of being a hypnotherapist myself.

One evening, I was browsing on the internet, and I decided to see if Paul was teaching a class. I saw that he was having a class in March, and I just knew that I had to take it. Right then it all clicked in. This was it. I felt a need to give back and offer people the same ability to discover what their purpose was in life. I don't know why I hadn't figured it out before. I was humbled and caught up in the miracle of the whole thing – the genius of a simple plan.

I registered online, and had my first class in mid-March in New York. Paul was teaching the class along with Jeff Cohen. I remember absorbing everything. I was like a sponge. Along with soaking up the information, I was overcome with what an amazing tool hypnotherapy is.

Those who choose it can find the experience that is right for them. To me that seemed to be the ideal way to help others.

Every day, I couldn't wait to get to class. While I sat in class, I would look around and wonder if everyone else was as captivated by the whole thing as I was. It was like reading Dr. Newton's book all over again – it was like food for my soul, and I was being given real, effective tools to be able to help people. What better way to help people get in touch with themselves and their purpose?

When people go to a hypnotherapist, it is usually the very last straw. Typically they have been everywhere else. Doctors. Chiropractors. Talk therapy. You name it. So, by the time they get to us, they are READY. And the thought of all of those people coming to me for help – instead of me having to find them. It was genius! I was overjoyed and overwhelmed.

In this environment, I excelled. I had a great understanding of what it felt like to be in trance, so I was already familiar with where we were going in the training. I was fearless, and all I saw were endless possibilities.

In order to pass the first class, you had to do only one thing. You had to understand a trance. You had to know how to put someone in a trance and bring them out of it. We learned about how hypnotherapy worked – the different states of consciousness and the different parts of the brain. The first training involved no therapy – just a trance. We also learned to be able to recognize when clients were and weren't in a trance, as well as different techniques for getting them there.

I felt like a kid in a candy store. I couldn't wait to get to the second part of the training.

We came back for the second part in April. In that session, we practiced on each other. Every day was observing, being hypnotized or doing hypnotherapy. People were terrified at first because it was new. The first time in front of a class was stressful but when we broke into groups, it was wonderful.

It was nice to be able to connect with Paul again. I wondered if this was what ALL meant – working together in school.

I completed the second part of the course with flying colors. I learned all of the basics of hypnotherapy: pre-talk, inductions, the code of hypnotherapists, confidentiality, all of it.

Because we were delving so deeply together, the class became a very trusting environment. A lot of things came up for a lot of people, and they were able to release emotions and roadblocks they'd held for a long time.

There were times when it was my turn to go under that I would ask ALL to please be quiet this time. He wasn't. He would pop up from time to time and make all kinds of revelations for my classmates. When there was a soul seeking answers, ALL stepped in and helped.

It became apparent that people wanted to hear what ALL had to say, and Paul and Jeff were quite accommodating. It took me a while to get comfortable with that. I worried that people might not want to hear what ALL had to say but ultimately I learned to trust that people don't receive information until they are ready for it, so who was I to deny anyone an opportunity for learning and growth? I was already helping people.

More Lives –
More Lessons

*History is merely a list of surprises. It can only
prepare us to be surprised yet again.*
~Kurt Vonnegat

CHAPTER 21

Life is a Stage

The earthly plane is like a play. It is a stage on which we learn the lessons necessary for the progress of our souls. Before we come into our incarnation as a human being, we cast the people who will come into our lives. It's all our choice – who we meet, who we love, the lessons we learn, and the obstacles that we encounter. We do this in order to progress as a soul entity.

Where you were born, when you were born, to whom you were born – these things are no accident. You chose it all, because you had a goal in mind.

The greatest gift you have ever received comes from every person you have encountered along your path. Each and every soul in the play of your life is here as a favor to you – not only the friends, not only the loves, but also those who toss you into turmoil, those you consider your enemies. They are all here because they love you, and they made a promise to you before you came here that they would help you learn, grow, and expand.

Each soul you encounter, each obstacle you must pass through – they are all here for you because you chose them to be here. Your life is of your design.

When you look at the intricacy of the connections, and you attempt to understand that with your mind, it is virtually impossible to grasp. If you instead attempt to feel these truths with your heart, then you will know that you are blessed with everything and everyone you could ever desire or need. You are blessed, whether you know it or not.

Feel inside of you. Find that space where you can feel this truth, and you will be overwhelmed with your connection to everyone and everything. In that space where you can feel the connection is where you truly reside, no matter what play you are staging for yourself on the earthly plane in this very moment.

Just as you are receiving gifts from others, your very presence in their lives is a gift to them. You made promises on the other side, too, and you are here fulfilling them. You are helping whether you know it or not. And the help is exponential. When you help one soul learn a lesson, that soul is enabled to help another and another.

Look at the challenges of your life. Not just the challenging situations, but also the challenging circumstances and people. It is in these challenges that you will find your path to yourself and ultimately, your path to the creator. You have given yourself whatever it takes to learn. Anything you need for your progress, you have provided it! What a blessing your challenges are. You have blessed yourself.

So what will you do? How will you assert your free will in a manner that supports this wonderful plan that you have laid out for yourself? It's a choice. Follow your path. Ignore your path. But the opportunities for lessons will keep coming because you gave yourself that gift. Here you are. What will you choose?

CHAPTER 22

Learning Integrity at the Hands of Jersey Mobsters

Integrity is not a conditional word. It doesn't blow in the wind or change with the weather. It is your inner image of yourself, and if you look in there and see a man who won't cheat, then you know he never will.
~John D. MacDonald

I died at the hands of Jersey mobsters. This is what I learned about myself one day at a clinic session in a Past Life Regression hypnotherapy workshop. We were practicing. I got to be the client.

That is how it works in hypnotherapy classes and workshops. You spend a lot of time putting each other under – and being put under. It's a great learning opportunity.

The day I learned I'd been killed by the mob, I was trying to discover why I suffered from allergies. This is what happens in a therapeutic session. You look at something that has a hold on you in this lifetime. It could be an ailment, an unhealthy relationship or something else. Each of these things is triggered by some kind of an emotion or energy that we hold onto which produces symptoms. I've suffered from severe allergies all of my life, and I was ready to get rid of them.

The therapist started to put me into a trance. She relaxed me and as I usually am, I was immediately in a trance state.

The first thing I noticed was that I couldn't move my legs. They felt heavy from my knees to my feet, as if something was sitting on them. This sensation of an inability to move was the first thing I sensed.

The therapist told me to focus in and see what was obstructing my legs. Now I realized that I couldn't move my legs because they were encased in cement.

The therapist then suggested that I pan out and look at the situation in order to get a sense of where I was and what was going on.

As she said that, I became instantly aware of the situation. I was sitting tied to a cane chair in the middle of a cold warehouse. My feet and legs were encased in cement. I was surrounded by three or four angry men. I could tell instantly that they were angry because of the dark energy that they emanated. The anger, violence and frustration of the men were all directed at me.

When the therapist asked why I was there in this situation, I knew. It came to me as a whole concept. The men's boss was angry with me because something had been taken from him. He felt I knew who did it but wouldn't tell. The men brought me to the warehouse to make me talk.

My friend in that life – my soul connection in this one – was the one I was protecting. The mob boss had stolen something from him, and he stole it back. He was righting a wrong but the mob boss didn't like that. He strongly suspected my friend had taken it, but he couldn't prove it. That was why I was there. I was the one with the information.

I knew my friend was in the right. I knew I had to protect my friend. So I didn't tell. I was tortured for three days by the men. They poured acid on my skin. They beat me. They hammered railroad spikes into my chest trying to get me to talk. They even tried electrocution.

Every night, they would leave expecting to find me dead the next day. Every morning, they would return for more torture. They kept expecting me to give in, and I wouldn't. This fueled their anger, and escalated their violence.

Each day, I grew progressively weaker. On the third morning, they came in and found me dead. This made them even angrier because they would now never get the information that they needed. The tossed me over the pier – cement, chair and all.

Right before I died, the person that I was in that moment came to a realization. The reason for my entire life – that one – was that I was there to learn integrity and honor. It was my purpose in that life to stand up for what was right, no matter what the personal consequences were. As soon as I realized that, I died.

There were other things that I knew during the session. I knew that the friend I was protecting was my soul connection in this life. I knew that the mob boss was my father – whose role in many of my incarnations has been that of the enforcer. He is with me now – as then – to make sure that I learn whatever lesson I need to in this life.

How does this tie into my life today? I deal constantly with asthma, eczema and allergies. I thought that the nails in my chest contributed to my asthma and the acid contributed to my eczema. And yet, this wasn't the main connection to this life.

All throughout my life as Lisa, I have felt that it was important to be truthful and honest. I have always stood up for the truth, no matter what. It was one thing that my father drilled into us as children. He always told me that I was responsible for the outcomes of my decisions – whether good or bad. This, I now know, came from that lifetime.

Have integrity – with yourself and with others. That is the lesson for my soul that came from dying at the hands of the New Jersey mob.

CHAPTER 23

Learning Forgiveness in Ancient Times

It seems that I have died violently more than once. I was stoned to death in a time that appeared to be Ancient Greece or Rome.

I learned this when I was being regressed in a Past Life Regression class. As always, the therapist asked what I'd like to look into, and I decided to learn about an old love interest in my present life. I also wanted to learn about my very unique relationship with my father, who has always been a force in my life. He is an iron fist in a velvet glove – making sure that I learn the lessons that I need to learn, but doing it with love.

So that was the intent of my session, and the therapist began to regress me. It happened quickly, and a scene opened up.

I was an older woman, dressed all in black. I was tired and tattered looking, as if I had been through much in my life. I was being stoned.

The people throwing the rocks at me were really angry. There were 60 or 70 of them – mostly men. They had huge rocks. I was sad, and very hurt that this was happening to me. I could see the big, giant rocks hitting me and feel the blood running down my head. The men were shouting things. At this point, I was still not sure why this was happening.

And then I got a sense of compassion for them. As they jeered at me, yelled at me and took my life from me one stone at a time, I was overcome with peace. They were killing me, and I could only feel forgiveness.

The therapist took me back in time to find out what had happened – what brought me to that place.

It was a time ruled by men. Very few women rose to a position of prominence, and yet, as a woman, I held a prominent position in a government that was similar to a council or parliament.

My best friend was the soul mate I had asked about. Before coming into this ancient lifetime, he knew what the outcome of my life would be, and he decided to be with me only for about 30 or 35 years. He said he had to leave after that because he could not bear to watch what would happen.

In that life, he was my best friend. We grew up together and both held prominent positions in government. When he was in his thirties, he got sick and died.

My father was also a very prominent person in this government. His energy was then – as it is now – wise, knowledgeable and powerful. The two of us were good friends and colleagues who had a tremendous amount of respect for one another.

As time went on, he began to worry that I would gain more power than him, and he launched a conspiracy against me. Ultimately he betrayed me, and I was ousted by the government.

Because I was well-revered as a politician, I was banished instead of being killed. I had to leave a life of comfort in the aristocracy and fend for myself.

For a long time, I was able to live in secrecy without people knowing who I was. Then my father gave away my identity. I was pushed into the middle of the city. I was stoned to death.

In that moment of dying, I realized that I had two choices. One – I could be angry because everything that had happened to me was not of my making. I knew that I had every right to curse them, but I wouldn't do it. Instead as I died, I prayed for them. I forgave them because they didn't know what they were doing. And in that moment, as I found forgiveness, I died.

In my moment of death, I knew what my entire life in that time was about – forgiveness in the face of betrayal. I have carried that into this lifetime. I've always been able to see the character of a person and see that they had a larger purpose. It is not an easy thing to do – watch another take advantage of you and turn the other cheek. But it was a lesson I learned in an ancient life, and it has been a source of strength in this one as I've pursued my path of helping others.

This is the lifetime in which I learned that my father is here for me as the enforcer. In that life, he made sure I would get the lesson of forgiveness in the face of that which appeared unforgivable.

CHAPTER 24

Everything I Need is Right Here

Everything you need you already have. You are complete right now, you are a whole, total person, not an apprentice person on the way to someplace else.
~Wayne Dyer

The first time I ever regressed a client into a past life, I learned that life gives you exactly what you need.

We were in class, getting ready to do our first Past Life Regression. I was both excited and curious about what might happen. When we worked in class in this manner, we would pair off in groups of three – one as the client, one as the hypnotherapist, and one as an observer. On this occasion, however, there were only two of us available to be in my group.

I was the hypnotherapist and she, a fellow student in class, was the client. As we started, my mind was filled with all of the things I'd learned to date.

I began the process of relaxing the client, and as I did, my natural instincts kicked in. It took about twenty minutes to get her to the relaxed state where we could begin transitioning to a past life.

As I regressed her, using imagery, I had her walk down stairs that led to a wonderful and relaxing place. As I took her first to a childhood memory, she was relaxed and the regression was smooth and easy. I told her that I would count backwards from three, and when I reached one she would be in a past life that was most significant to this moment for her learning right now.

Immediately she began to thrash around and gasp for air. She was having what is referred to as an abreaction. An abreaction is where the body reacts physically to the trauma of a past life and releases the energy or emotion from the memory it is reliving.

It was immediately obvious that my client was drowning. Her reaction was strong – thrashing and gasping. She was visibly struggling. As a first time therapist, this reaction can be very alarming but surprisingly (or perhaps not surprisingly), my instincts kicked in. I knew I needed to help her to objectify what she was experiencing by moving to a safe place from which she could view the events as an observer while still understanding and being connected to the emotions. Before I could do that, however, she progressed to the death scene in that life. After experiencing the death of that life she became calmer although still somewhat shaken.

The client expressed her desire to gain understanding of what she had just experienced. I then began counting her back and deepening her trance state. Again she reverted back to the abreaction and began thrashing and gasping as if she were drowning. She was in obvious pain, crying and talking about the water.

I moved her to a safe place to avoid the pain of the drowning and allow her to get calm and regroup so the she could begin to view the circumstances leading to the death. At this time, I decided to regress her back to fifteen minutes before the death scene because I wanted to help her find the understanding she needed from this life.

There was a reason that she had regressed to this lifetime and this moment, and she needed to find that integral piece of understanding in this experience that would help her. My plan was to ease her forward slowly to the moment of her death so that she could see what she came here to see.

She was still very tense and apprehensive. Speaking in the voice of a young boy, she described what she saw.

I suggested she get a sense of how old she was and where in time she was. The story emerged that she was a young male who was perhaps fourteen years old. She, the client, who was male in that life was on a ship with her brother.

She and her brother were hands on a ship in the late 1700s. She began to describe her surroundings and clothing.

She seemed comfortable with her understanding of her life and recognition of her brother. Her brother's soul was familiar to her and she recognized him and knew that they had shared many lives together. I progressed her forward towards the time of her death in that life. This time, her abreaction was stronger than the first time.

She was in charge of the food supply and had mishandled the food in some way – something minor. The captain on the ship, who wasn't a very nice person, was angry with the young boy. The boy's brother came to his defense and told the captain to leave the boy alone. The brother and the captain began arguing and a fight ensued.

The client was very agitated as she told this story – so much so that one of the instructors came and stood behind me to make sure that I didn't need any help.

I was still trying to give her suggestions about stepping back and watching the scene as an objective observer rather than being involved in it, but her emotion was extremely high. She was holding on to the emotion and pain of the moment in a big way.

In the middle of the fight between the captain and the brother, the young boy stepped into the middle and somehow got kicked in the stomach. When this happened in the regression, my client doubled over in pain and started gasping for breath. She was having yet another abreaction.

I moved her forward to what happened next. The captain somehow got past the boy's brother and in the ruckus he threw her overboard into the water. She immediately started gasping and thrashing. I had her rise above the scene and instructed her to separate herself from the experience.

The boy died in the water. It was an extremely difficult but successful regression. She worked through it and got what she needed out of it, which was a release of the pain and grief over the situation that she had carried for many lifetimes to the present day, This experience was a confirmation of the devotion and loyalty that souls can have for one another that transcends our illusion of physical limitations bound to one body, one life, and one time.

As a hypnotherapist, I always get as much out of a session as my client does. Within each past life regression lies an opportunity for wisdom that is there for me, as well.

This session, as my first past life session, was extremely difficult and called for advanced techniques with which I'd had little or no experience. The more chaotic my client appeared to be, the more I naturally slipped into focus.

As a hypnotherapy student, you think you know what you'll do in difficult situations but you can never be sure exactly how you'll react. After this very first session, what I learned is that with the help of my guides, my instincts and my training, I am able to handle any situation that arises in hypnotherapy.

This, my first session as a past life regression hypnotherapist, showed me that no matter what arises in a session, I will be personally equipped and guided to handle it. The session gave me exactly what I needed at the moment that I needed it.

The session has laid a foundation for me that allows me to go into every situation as a hypnotherapist confident that my clients will get what they need, and so will I. It enabled me to have confidence that what I do makes a difference, and that I am using my life exactly in the way that it should be used. For that I am grateful, and in that, I am blessed.

AFTERWORD

What Really Matters

*Your work is to discover your world and
then with all your heart give yourself to it.*
~Buddha

Live this life. It is why you are here – master the lessons that you agreed to learn.

Past lives are interesting, and in them there is information that can help you to move forward and live fully and completely in the present.

There is tremendous courage involved in being present in your life. The challenge is to be fully and wholly devoted to each moment and tuned in to your inner guidance and your soul's purpose. You have the courage. you've done it before in other lifetimes.

No life is a wasted. You are here for a reason. The reason may not be clear to you right now, and that's okay. As you become present and aware of who you really are, as you start to listen to the yearnings of your soul, as you tune into and trust the guidance your life's purpose will unfold.

Be here, now. Live this life to best of your ability. After all... it's why you came.

ACKNOWLEDGEMENTS

To my parents Harold & Mattie; for without them "**this**" life would not be possible. Love you always!

To **all** of the wonderful beings who have touched my life, I thank you from the depths of my soul. It is with great gratitude I carry the many lessons you have given me to touch others.

59262009R00066

Made in the USA
Middletown, DE
11 August 2019